Common Tasks in GIMP 2.8

By

U. C-Abel Books

COPYRIGHT

All Rights Reserved

First Edition: 2017

Copyright @ U. C-Abel Books. ISBN-13: 978-1979981828

This book, **Common Tasks in GIMP 2.8** *with ISBN-13: 978-1979981828, has been licensed by copyright proprietors, therefore producing it in whatever way or creating an alternate format without a written permission from the copyright holder is an infringement of copyright and violators will be punished.*

However, some parts of this book is freely available at www.gimp.org. Visit their website if you want it for any purpose but make sure you read their legal documentation and for peace sake, don't copy from this particular book.

ISBN-13: 978-1979981828

ISBN-10: 1979981825

Published by U. C-Abel Books.

INTRODUCTION

GIMP (GNU Image Manipulation Program) is a free multi-platform photo manipulation tool. The GIMP is suitable for a variety of image manipulation tasks, including photo retouching, image composition, and image construction. It works on the following platforms: GNU/Linux™, Apple Mac OS X™, Microsoft Windows™, OpenBSD™, NetBSD™, FreeBSD™, Solaris™, SunOS™, AIX™, HP-UX™, Tru64™, Digital UNIX™, OSF/1™, IRIX™, OS/2™, and BeOS™.

The GIMP is a Free Software application covered by the General Public License [GPL]. The GPL provides users with the freedom to access and alter the source code that makes up computer programs.

In sincerity, we never thought of selling this book or bringing it to the public at first. We only compiled it to help ourselves use this image manipulation program called GIMP better, and as well have something we can run to when a challenge shows up.

The main purpose of this publication is to help people who want to be better in what they do with GIMP 2.8.

This book is for users of GIMP (Beginner, Medium or Expert) and for any profession: Graphics Designers, Photographers, Painting Artists, or any other category so far as image manipulation with GIMP is concerned.

Get in love with GIMP; manipulate your image in whatsoever manner that seems good to you.

Happy GIMPing!

TABLE OF CONTENTS

Chapter 1: Introduction 6
   1. Welcome to GIMP 6
   1.1. Authors 6
   1.2. The GIMP Help system 7
   1.3. Features and Capabilities 7
   2. What's New in GIMP 2.8? 8

Chapter 2: Fire up the GIMP 20
   1. Running GIMP 20
   2. 1.1. Known Platforms 20
   3. 1.2. Language 21
   4. 1.3. Command Line Arguments 22
   5. 2. Starting GIMP the first time 25
   6. 2.1. Finally 26

Chapter 3: First Steps with Wilber 27
   1. Basic Concepts 27
   2. Main Windows 32
   2.1. The Toolbox 37
   2.2. Image Window 39
   2.3. Dialogs and Docking 45
   3. Undoing 56
   3.1. Things That Cannot be Undone 57
   4. Common Tasks 59
   4.1. Intention 59
   4.2. Change the Size of an Image for the screen 60
   4.3. Change the Size of an Image for print 63
   4.4. Compressing Images 64
   4.5. Crop An Image 68
   4.6. Find Info About Your Image 71

4.7. Change the Mode 72
   4.8. Flip An Image 75
   4.9. Rotate An Image 76
   4.10. Separating an Object From Its Background 78
   5. How to Draw Straight Lines 83
   5.1. Intention 83
   5.2. Examples 88

Chapter 4: Getting Unstuck **90**
   1. Getting Unstuck 90
   1.1. Stuck! 90
   1.2. Common Causes of GIMP Non-Responsiveness 90

How to Get Your 939-Page GIMP Book **96**

CHAPTER 1. INTRODUCTION

1. Welcome to GIMP

GIMP is a multi-platform photo manipulation tool. GIMP is an acronym for GNU Image Manipulation Program. The GIMP is suitable for a variety of image manipulation tasks, including photo retouching, image composition, and image construction.

GIMP has many capabilities. It can be used as a simple paint program, an expert quality photo retouching program, an online batch processing system, a mass production image renderer, an image format converter, etc.

GIMP is expandable and extensible. It is designed to be augmented with plug-ins and extensions to do just about anything. The advanced scripting interface allows everything from the simplest task to the most complex image manipulation procedures to be easily scripted.

One of The GIMP's strengths is its free availability from many sources for many operating systems. Most GNU/Linux distributions include The GIMP as a standard application. The GIMP is also available for other operating systems such as Microsoft Windows™ or Apple's Mac OS X™ (Darwin). The GIMP is a Free Software application covered by the General Public License [GPL]. The GPL provides users with the freedom to access and alter the source code that makes up computer programs.

1.1. Authors

The first version of the GIMP was written by Peter Mattis and Spencer Kimball. Many other developers have contributed more recently, and thousands have provided support and testing. GIMP releases are currently being orchestrated by Sven Neumann and Mitch Natterer and the other members of the GIMP-Team.

1.2. The GIMP Help system

The GIMP Documentation Team and other users have provided you with the information necessary to understand how to use GIMP. The User Manual is an important part of this help. The current version is on the web site of the Documentation Team [GIMP-DOCS] in HTML format. The HTML version is also available as context sensitive help (if you installed it) while using GIMP by pressing the **F1** key. Help on specific menu items can be accessed by pressing the **F1** key while the mouse pointer is focused on the menu item. Read on to begin your GIMP journey.

1.3. Features and Capabilities

The following list is a short overview of some of the features and capabilities which GIMP offers you:

- A full suite of painting tools including brushes, a pencil, an airbrush, cloning, etc.
- Tile-based memory management, so image size is limited only by available disk space
- Sub-pixel sampling for all paint tools for high-quality anti-aliasing
- Full Alpha channel support for working with transparency
- Layers and channels
- A procedural database for calling internal GIMP functions from external programs, such as Script-Fu
- Advanced scripting capabilities
- Multiple undo/redo (limited only by disk space)
- Transformation tools including rotate, scale, shear and flip
- Support for a wide range of file formats, including GIF, JPEG, PNG, XPM, TIFF, TGA, MPEG, PS, PDF, PCX, BMP and many others
- Selection tools, including rectangle, ellipse, free, fuzzy, bezier and intelligent scissors
- Plug-ins that allow for the easy addition of new file formats and new effect filters.

2. What's New in GIMP 2.8?

GIMP 2.8 is another important release from a development point of view, even more that it was for 2.6. It features a big change to the user interface addressing one of the most often received complaints: the lack of a single window mode. Moreover the integration effort of GEGL library had taken a big step forward, reaching more than 90% of the GIMP core, a new powerful transformation tool, layer groups, new common options, new brushes, improved text tool, and more.

User Interface

New single window mode

> With this new feature it will be possible to work with all the GIMP dialogs inside one big window, usually with the image(s) centered inside. No more floating panels or toolbox but the dialogs could be arranged inside this single window. This mode could be enabled or disabled all the time, even while working, and the option will be remembered through the sessions.

Figure 1.1. The new look of the single window mode

New file save workflow

> Now Save and Save as work only with xcf formats. If you want to export an image in another format, say jpg or png, you have to explicitly Export it. This enhances the workflow and lets you simply overwrite the original file or export to various other formats.
>
> **Figure 1.2. The new image workflow**

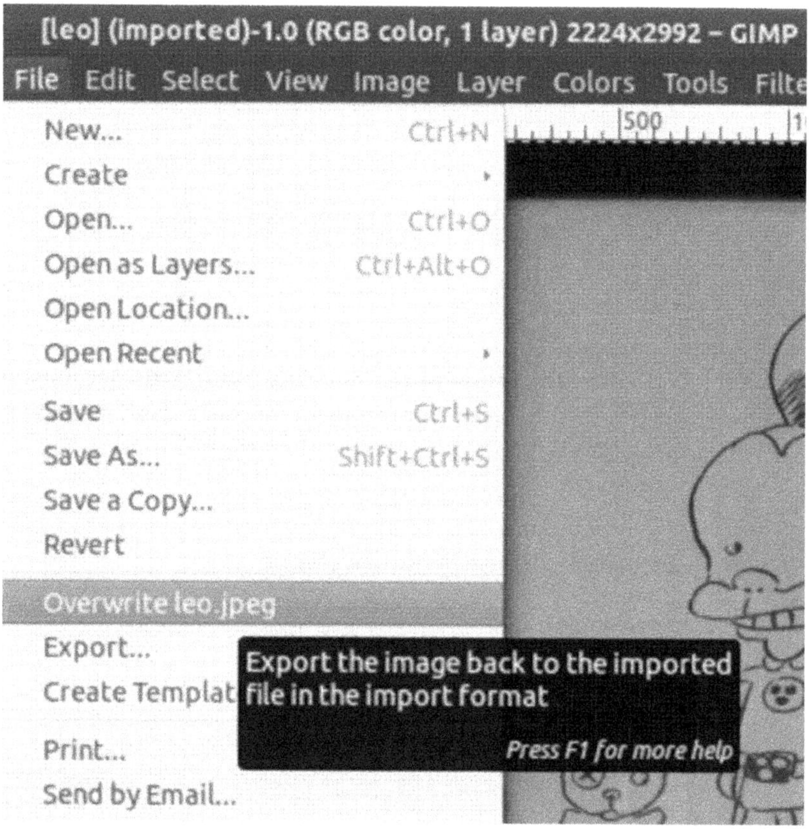

New image bar

> A new useful image bar comes with the single window mode, which lets you switch easily between open images through the means of a tab bar with image thumbnails.

Figure 1.3. The new image bar

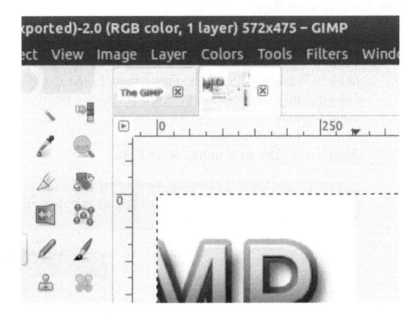

New arrangement options

GIMP will make users working with two screens (one for dialogs, the other for images) happy: now it is possible to arrange the dialogs one over the other, in tabs and in columns too.

Figure 1.4. Multi column docks

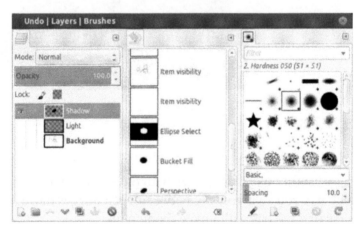

New resources tags

> GIMP Brushes, Gradients, Pattern and Palettes can be filtered and searched via tags. Tags are text labels that the user can assign to resources. With Tags the user can easily find the resources by means of an input text box. Tags can be manually assigned by the user with the same input box used for searching tags, or they can be automatically tagged using the directory name of the imported items.
>
> **Figure 1.5. Resource tags**

Simple math in size entries

> Enhancements have also been made to the size entry widget, which is used for inputting most of the x, y, width, height parameters. For example, in the scale dialog it is now possible to write "50%" in the Width field to scale the image to 50% of the width. Expressions such as "30in + 40px" and "4 * 5.4in" work, too.

Figure 1.6. Math size entries

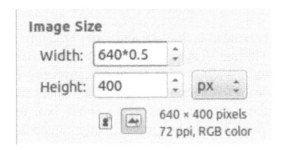

Minor changes

- The new "Lock Pixels" option in the layers dialog can avoid undesired painting on a layer when working with several layers.

Figure 1.7. The new Lock Pixels option

- Now you can move between images in single and multi-window mode using the shortcuts **Ctrl+PageUp/PageDown** or **Alt+Number**.
- Add support for F2 to rename items in lists.

- You can now **Alt+Click** on layers in the Layers dialog to create a selection from it. Add, subtract and intersect modifiers **Click, Shift** and **Ctrl+Shift** keys work too. This makes it easy to compose contents of a layer based on the contents of other layers, without detours.
- Since the keyboard shortcuts **Ctrl+E** and **Ctrl+Shift+E** have been redirected to image export mechanisms, new keyboard shortcuts have been setup for "Shrink Wrap" and "Fit in Window", namely **Ctrl+J** and **Ctrl+Shift+J** respectively.
- Added Windows → Hide docks menu item that does what "Tab" does and also displays its state, which is now persistent across sessions, too.
- The layer modes have been rearranged into more logical and useful groups based on the effect they have on layers. Layer modes that make the layer lighter are in one group, layer modes that make the layer darker in another group, and so forth.
- In multi-window mode, you can now close the Toolbox without quitting GIMP.
- Allow binding arbitrary actions to extra mouse buttons.
- Now it is possible to change the application language directly from the preference menu.

Tools, Filters and Plug-ins

A new tool: Cage Transform

> With this new tool is now possible to create custom bending of a selection just moving control points. This is the result of one of our Google Summer of Code 2010 students.

Figure 1.8. Cage Transform

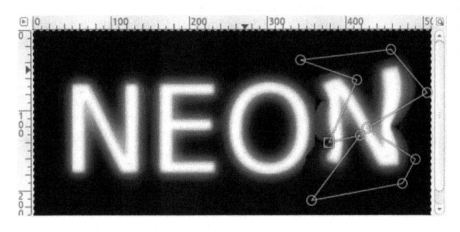

Improved Text Tool

The text tool has been enhanced to support on canvas text writing and make possible changing the attributes of a single char.

Figure 1.9. Improved text tool

New layer groups

It is now possible to group set of layers and treat them like an entity. It is possible to switch a group on or off and to move the group in the layers dialog. It is easy to add / remove existing layers to a group or to create / delete a layer inside the group and it is even possible to create embedded groups of groups. It is possible to apply a layer mode to a group as you do with a single layer. All this greatly improves the workflow with complex multilayer images making them easier to manage.

Figure 1.10. New layer groups

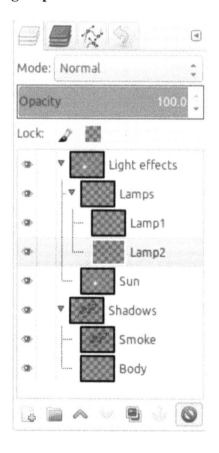

Rotating brushes

Brushes can now be rotated at will, acting on the brush option "Angle".

Figure 1.11. Rotating brushes

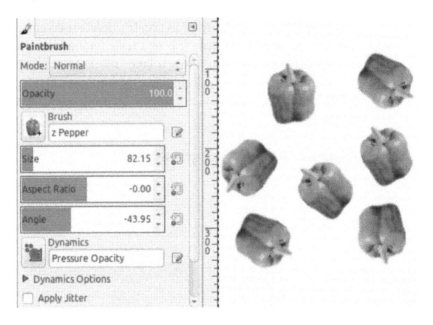

Minor changes

- The default Quick Mask color is now configurable.
- The RTL mode (right to left writing) has been improved in the Text tool.
- You can specify the written language in the Text Tool. This helps choosing an appropriate font, or appropriate glyphs for the selected language.
- Added optional diagonal guides to the crop tool.
- Added "Rule of fifths" crop guide overlay.
- A Cairo based PDF exporter has been implemented. Although being somewhat simplistic, the exporter saves text, embedding fonts into the final PDF file, and attempts to convert bitmaps to vector objects.
- Brush dynamics improved.
- Added plug-in for loading JPEG2000 images.

- Added plug-ins for X11 Mouse Cursor import and export support.
- Added fundamental OpenRaster (.ora) import and export support.
- Added RGB565 support to the csource plug-in.
- Added a new "Create" command that allows loading a Web page directly into GIMP using Webkit.

Under the Hood

GEGL

The porting of the GIMP core towards the new high bit-depth and non-destructive editing GEGL. GEGL library has taken big steps and now more than 90% of the task is already finished.

In addition to porting color operations to GEGL, an experimental GEGL Operation tool has been added, found in the Tools menu. It enables applying GEGL operations to an image and it gives on-canvas previews of the results. The screenshot below shows this for a Gaussian Blur.

Figure 1.12. GEGL operation

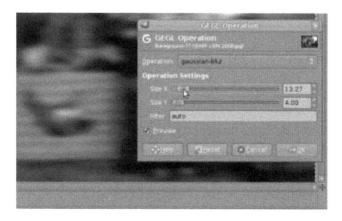

Cairo porting

Started with GIMP version 2.6, all tools rendering on canvas is now completely ported to CAIRO. It provides smooth antialiased graphics and improves GIMP look. Some plug-ins have been upgraded to Cairo as well. Additionally all tools now use an on-canvas progress indicator instead of the one in the statusbar.

Figure 1.13. Progress indicator

Miscellaneous

License change

The GIMP license has been changed to (L)GPLv3+.

New script API

- A lot of GIMP APIs have been rebuilt to simplify developing new scripts.
- To further enhances scripting abilities, API changes to support layer groups have been made.

Backwards Compatibility

To allow migrating from the old tools presets system to the new one, there is a Python script, which you can download from the GIMP wiki site. However, the old tools presets are not 100% convertible to the new tool presets. For instance, brush scale from 2.6 can't be converted to brush size in 2.8.

Known Problems

Working with graphics tablets could be problematic due to the GTK+2 library in use. If in this case either use the older version 2.6 or wait for the upcoming version 3.0 for the full GTK+3 support.

CHAPTER 2. FIRE UP THE GIMP

1. Running GIMP

Most often, you start GIMP either by clicking on an icon (if your system is set up to provide you with one), or by typing **gimp** on a command line. If you have multiple versions of GIMP installed, you may need to type **gimp-2.8** to get the latest version. You can, if you want, give a list of image files on the command line after the program name, and they will automatically be opened by GIMP as it starts. It is also possible, though, to open files from within GIMP once it is running.

Most operating systems support file associations, which associates a class of files (as determined by their filename extension, such as .jpg) with a corresponding application (such as GIMP). When image files are properly "associated" to GIMP, you can double click on an image to open it in GIMP.

1.1. Known Platforms

The GIMP is the most widely supported image manipulation available today. The platforms on which GIMP is known to work include:

GNU/Linux™, Apple Mac OS X™, Microsoft Windows™, OpenBSD™, NetBSD™, FreeBSD™, Solaris™, SunOS™, AIX™, HP-UX™, Tru64™, Digital UNIX™, OSF/1™, IRIX™, OS/2™, and BeOS™.

The GIMP is easily ported to other operating systems because of its source code availability. For further information visit the GIMP developers homepage. GIMP-DEV.

1.2. Language

GIMP automatically detects and uses the system language. In the unlikely event that language detection fails, or if you just want to use a different language, since GIMP-2.8, you can do so through: Edit → Preferences → Interface.

You can also use:

Under Linux

> *In LINUX*: in console mode, type **LANGUAGE=en gimp** or **LANG=en gimp** replacing en by fr, de, ... according to the language you want. Background: Using **LANGUAGE=en** sets an environment variable for the executed program **gimp**.

Under Windows XP

> Control Panel → System → Advanced → Environment button in "System Variables" area: Add button: Enter LANG for Name and fr or de... for Value. Watch out! You have to click on three successive OK to validate your choice.
>
> If you change languages often, you can create a batch file to change the language. Open NotePad. Type the following commands (for french for instance):
>
> **set lang=fr**
> **start gimp-2.8.exe**
>
> Save this file as GIMP-FR.BAT (or another name, but always with a .BAT extension). Create a shortcut and drag it to your desktop.

Another possibility: Start → Programs → GTK Runtime Environment Then Select language and select the language you want in the drop-down list.

Under Apple Mac OS X

From System Preferences, click on the International icon. In the Language tab, the desired language should be the first in the list.

Another GIMP instance

Use **-n** to run multiple instances of GIMP. For example, use **gimp-2.8** to start GIMP in the default system language, and **LANGUAGE=en gimp-2.8 -n** to start another instance of GIMP in English; this is very useful for translators.

1.3. Command Line Arguments

Although arguments are not required when starting GIMP, the most common arguments are shown below. On a Unix system, you can use **man gimp** for a complete list.

Command line arguments must be in the command line that you use to start GIMP as **gimp-2.8 [OPTION...] [FILE|URI...]**.

-?, --help

Display a list of all commandline options.

--help-all

Show all help options.

--help-gtk

Show GTK+ Options.

-v, --version

> Print the GIMP version and exit.

--license

> Show license information and exit.

--verbose

> Show detailed start-up messages.

-n, --new-instance

> Start a new GIMP instance.

-a, --as-new

> Open images as new.

-i, --no-interface

> Run without a user interface.

-d, --no-data

> Do not load patterns, gradients, palettes, or brushes. Often useful in non-interactive situations where start-up time is to be minimized.

-f, --no-fonts

> Do not load any fonts. This is useful to load GIMP faster for scripts that do not use fonts, or to find problems related to malformed fonts that hang GIMP.

-s, --no-splash

> Do not show the splash screen while starting.

--no-shm

Do not use shared memory between GIMP and plugins.

--no-cpu-accel

Do not use special CPU acceleration functions. Useful for finding or disabling buggy accelerated hardware or functions.

--session=*name*

Use a different sessionrc for this GIMP session. The given session name is appended to the default sessionrc filename.

--gimprc=filename

Use an alternative gimprc instead of the default one. The gimprc file contains a record of your preferences. Useful in cases where plugins paths or machine specs may be different.

--system-gimprc=*filename*

Use an alternate system gimprc file.

-b, --batch=*commands*

Execute the set of commands non-interactively. The set of commands is typically in the form of a script that can be executed by one of the GIMP scripting extensions. When the command is -, commands are read from standard input.

--batch-interpreter=*proc*

Specify the procedure to use to process batch commands. The default procedure is Script-Fu.

--console-messages

Do not popup dialog boxes on errors or warnings. Print the messages on the console instead.

--pdb-compat-mode=*mode*

>   PDB compatibility mode (off|on|warn).

--stack-trace-mode=*mode*

>   Debug in case of a crash (never|query|always).

--debug-handlers

>   Enable non-fatal debugging signal handlers. Useful for GIMP debugging.

--g-fatal-warnings

>   Make all warnings fatal. Useful for debug.

--dump-gimprc

>   Output a gimprc file with default settings. Useful if you messed up the gimprc file.

--display=*display*

>   Use the designated X display (does not apply to all platforms).

2. Starting GIMP the first time

When first run, GIMP performs a series of steps to configure options and directories. The configuration process creates a subdirectory in your home directory called .gimp-2.8. All of the configuration information is stored in this directory. If you remove or rename the directory, GIMP will repeat the initial configuration process, creating a new .gimp-2.8 directory. Use this capability to explore different configuration options without destroying your existing installation, or to recover if your configuration files are damaged.

2.1. Finally . . .

Just a couple of suggestions before you start, though: First, GIMP provides tips you can read at any time using the menu command Help → Tip of the Day. The tips provide information that is considered useful, but not easy to learn by experimenting; so they are worth reading. Please read the tips when you have the time. Second, if at some point you are trying to do something, and GIMP seems to have suddenly stopped functioning, the section Getting Unstuck may help you out. Happy Gimping!

CHAPTER 3. FIRST STEPS WITH WILBER

1. Basic Concepts

Figure 3.1. Wilber, the GIMP mascot

The Wilber_Construction_Kit (in src/images/) allows you to give the mascot a different appearance. It is the work of Tuomas Kuosmanen (tigertATgimp.org).

This section provides a brief introduction to the basic concepts and terminology used in GIMP. The concepts presented here are explained in much greater depth elsewhere. With a few exceptions, we have avoided cluttering this section with a lot of links and cross-references: everything mentioned here is so high-level that you can easily locate it in the index.

Images

> Images are the basic entities used by GIMP. Roughly speaking, an "image" corresponds to a single file, such as a TIFF or JPEG file. You can also think of an image as corresponding to a single display window (although in truth it

is possible to have multiple windows all displaying the same image). It is not possible to have a single window display more than one image, though, or for an image to have no window displaying it.

A GIMP image may be quite a complicated thing. Instead of thinking of it as a sheet of paper with a picture on it, think of it as more like a stack of sheets, called "layers". In addition to a stack of layers, a GIMP image may contain a selection mask, a set of channels, and a set of paths. In fact, GIMP provides a mechanism for attaching arbitrary pieces of data, called "parasites", to an image.

In GIMP, it is possible to have many images open at the same time. Although large images may use many megabytes of memory, GIMP uses a sophisticated tile-based memory management system that allows GIMP to handle very large images gracefully. There are limits, however, and having more memory available may improve system performance.

Layers

If a simple image can be compared to a single sheet of paper, an image with layers is likened to a sheaf of transparent papers stacked one on top of the other. You can draw on each paper, but still see the content of the other sheets through the transparent areas. You can also move one sheet in relation to the others. Sophisticated GIMP users often deal with images containing many layers, even dozens of them. Layers need not be opaque, and they need not cover the entire extent of an image, so when you look at an image's display, you may see more than just the top layer: you may see elements of many layers.

Resolution

Digital images comprise of a grid of square elements of varying colors, called pixels. Each image has a pixel size, such as 900 pixels wide by 600 pixels high. But pixels don't have a set size in physical space. To set up an image for printing, we use a value called resolution, defined as the ratio between an image's size in pixels and its physical size (usually in inches) when it is printed on paper. Most file formats (but not all) can save this value, which is expressed as ppi — pixels per inch. When printing a file, the resolution value determines the size the image will have on paper, and as a result, the physical size of the pixels. The same 900x600 pixel image may be printed as a small 3x2" card with barely noticeable pixels — or as a large poster with large, chunky pixels. Images imported from cameras and mobile devices tend to have a resolution value attached to the file. The value is usually 72 or 96ppi. It is important to realize that this value is arbitrary and was chosen for historic reasons. You can always change the resolution value inside GIMP — this has no effect on the actual image pixels. Furthermore, for uses such as displaying images on line, on mobile devices, television or video games — in short, any use that is not print — the resolution value is meaningless and is ignored, and instead the image is usually displayed so that each image pixel conforms to one screen pixel.

Channels

A Channel is a single component of a pixel's color. For a colored pixel in GIMP, these components are usually Red, Green, Blue and sometimes transparency (Alpha). For a Grayscale image, they are Gray and Alpha and for an Indexed color image, they are Indexed and Alpha.

The entire rectangular array of any one of the color components for all of the pixels in an image is also referred to as a Channel. You can see these color channels with the Channels dialog.

When the image is displayed, GIMP puts these components together to form the pixel colors for the screen, printer, or other output device. Some output devices may use different channels from Red, Green and Blue. If they do, GIMP's channels are converted into the appropriate ones for the device when the image is displayed.

Channels can be useful when you are working on an image which needs adjustment in one particular color. For example, if you want to remove "red eye" from a photograph, you might work on the Red channel.

You can look at channels as masks which allow or restrict the output of the color that the channel represents. By using Filters on the channel information, you can create many varied and subtle effects on an image. A simple example of using a Filter on the color channels is the Channel Mixer filter.

In addition to these channels, GIMP also allows you to create other channels (or more correctly, Channel Masks), which are displayed in the lower part of the Channels dialog. You can create a New Channel or save a selection to a channel (mask). See the glossary entry on Masks for more information about Channel Masks.

Selections

Often when modify an image, you only want a part of the image to be affected. The "selection" mechanism makes this possible. Each image has its own selection, which you normally see as a moving dashed line separating the selected parts from the unselected parts (the so-called "marching ants"). Actually this is a bit misleading: selection in GIMP is graded, not all-or-nothing, and really the selection is represented by a full-fledged grayscale channel. The dashed line that you normally see is simply a contour line at the 50%-selected level. At any time, though, you can visualize the selection channel in all its glorious detail by toggling the **QuickMask** button.

A large component of learning how to use GIMP effectively is acquiring the art of making good selections—selections that contain exactly what you need and nothing more. Because

Your Details

ANDREW SQUIRE
117 jarden
letchworth
Hertfordshire
SG6 2NZ

Order date: 18/08/2018
Order reference: ESSUK-38715315
Dispatch note: 20180822951101

Your Order

ISBN	Title	Quantity
9781979981828	Common Tasks in Gimp 2.8	1

For returns information visit wordery.com/returns. Please keep this receipt for your records.

Get 10% off your next order at
Wordery.com. Use code
WELCOME10 at the checkout.
#HappyReading

20180822951101

selection-handling is so centrally important, GIMP provides many tools for doing it: an assortment of selection-making tools, a menu of selection operations, and the ability to switch to Quick Mask mode, in which you can treat the selection channel as though it were a color channel, thereby "painting the selection".

Undoing

When you make mistakes, you can undo them. Nearly everything you can do to an image is undoable. In fact, you can usually undo a substantial number of the most recent things you did, if you decide that they were misguided. GIMP makes this possible by keeping a history of your actions. This history consumes memory, though, so undoability is not infinite. Some actions use very little undo memory, so that you can do dozens of them before the earliest ones are deleted from this history; other types of actions require massive amounts of undo memory. You can configure the amount of memory GIMP allows for the undo history of each image, but in any situation, you should always be able to undo at least your 2-3 most recent actions. (The most important action that is not undoable is closing an image. For this reason, GIMP asks you to confirm that you really want to close the image if you have made any changes to it.)

Plug-ins

Many, probably most, of the things that you do to an image in GIMP are done by the GIMP application itself. However, GIMP also makes extensive use of "plug-ins", which are external programs that interact very closely with GIMP, and are capable of manipulating images and other GIMP objects in very sophisticated ways. Many important plug-ins are bundled with GIMP, but there are also many available by other means. In fact, writing plug-ins (and scripts) is the easiest way for people not on the GIMP development team to add new capabilities to GIMP.

All of the commands in the Filters menu, and a substantial number of commands in other menus, are actually implemented as plug-ins.

Scripts

In addition to plug-ins, which are programs written in the C language, GIMP can also make use of scripts. The largest number of existing scripts are written in a language called Script-Fu, which is unique to GIMP (for those who care, it is a dialect of the Lisp-like language called Scheme). It is also possible to write GIMP scripts in Python or Perl. These languages are more flexible and powerful than Script-Fu; their disadvantage is that they depend on software that does not automatically come packaged with GIMP, so they are not guaranteed to work correctly in every GIMP installation.

2. Main Windows

The GIMP user interface is now available in two modes:

- multi-window mode,
- single window mode.

When you open GIMP for the first time, it opens in multi-window mode by default. You can enable single-window mode through Windows → >Single-Window Mode) in the image menu bar. After quitting GIMP with this option enabled, GIMP will start in single-window mode next time.

Multi-Window Mode

Figure 3.2. A screenshot illustrating the multi-window mode.

The screenshot above shows the most basic arrangement of GIMP windows that can be used effectively.

You can notice two panels, left and right, and an image window in middle. A second image is partially masked. The left panel collects Toolbox and Tool Options dialog together. The right panel collects layers, channels, paths, undo history dialogs together in a multi-tab dock, brushes, patterns and gradients dialogs together in another dock below. You can move these panels on screen. You can also mask them using the **Tab** key.

1. *The Main Toolbox:* Contains a set of icon buttons used to select tools. By default, it also contains the foreground and background colors. You can add brush, pattern, gradient and active image icons. Use Edit → Preferences → Toolbox to enable, or disable the extra items.

2. *Tool options:* Docked below the main Toolbox is a Tool Options dialog, showing options for the currently selected tool (in this case, the Move tool).
3. *Image windows:* Each image open in GIMP is displayed in a separate window. Many images can be open at the same time, limited by only the system resources. Before you can do anything useful in GIMP, you need to have at least one image window open. The image window holds the Menu of the main commands of GIMP (File, Edit, Select...), which you can also get by right-clicking on the window.

   An image can be bigger than the image window. In that case, GIMP displays the image in a reduced zoom level which allows to see the full image in the image window. If you turn to the 100% zoom level, scroll bars appear, allowing you to pan across the image.
4. The *Layers, Channels, Paths, Undo History* dock — note that the dialogs in the dock are tabs. The Layers tab is open: it shows the layer structure of the currently active image, and allows it to be manipulated in a variety of ways. It is possible to do a few very basic things without using the Layers dialog, but even moderately sophisticated GIMP users find it indispensable to have the Layers dialog available at all times.
5. *Brushes/Patterns/Gradients:* The docked dialog below the layer dialog shows the dialogs (tabs) for managing brushes, patterns and gradients.

Dialog and dock managing is described in Section 2.3, "Dialogs and Docking".

Single Window Mode

Figure 3.3. A screenshot illustrating the single-window mode.

You find the same elements, with differences in their management:

- Left and right panels are fixed; you can't move them. But you can decrease or increase their width. If you reduce the width of a multi-tab dock, there may be not enough place for all tabs; then arrow-heads appear allowing you to scroll through tabs.

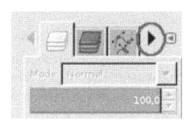

As in multi-window mode, you can mask these panels using the **Tab** key.

- The image window occupies all space between both panels.

   When several images are open, a new bar appears above the image window, with a tab for every image. You can navigate between images by clicking on tabs or either using **Ctrl+PageUp or PageDown** or **Alt+Number**. "Number" is tab number; you must use the number keys of the upper line of your keyboard, not that of keypad (Alt-shift necessary for some national keyboards).

This is a minimal setup. There are over a dozen other types of dialogs used by GIMP for various purposes, but users typically open them when they need them and close them when they are done. Knowledgeable users generally keep the Toolbox (with Tool Options) and Layers dialog open at all times. The Toolbox is essential to many GIMP operations. The Tool Options section is actually a separate dialog, shown docked to the Main Toolbox in the screenshot. Knowledgeable users almost always have it set up this way: it is very difficult to use tools effectively without being able to see how their options are set. The Layers dialog comes into play when you work with an image with multiple layers: after you advance beyond the most basic stages of GIMP expertise, this means *almost always*. And of course it helps to display the images you're editing on the screen; if you close the image window before saving your work, GIMP will ask you whether you want to close the file.

Note

If your GIMP layout is lost, your arrangement is easy to recover using Windows → Recently Closed Docks; the Windows menu command is only available while an image is open. To add, close, or detach a tab from a dock, click

36

in the upper right corner of a dialog. This opens the Tab menu. Select Add Tab, Close Tab , or Detach Tab.

The following sections walk you through the components of each of the windows shown in the screenshot, explaining what they are and how they work. Once you have read them, plus the section describing the basic structure of GIMP images, you should have learned enough to use GIMP for a wide variety of basic image manipulations. You can then look through the rest of the manual at your leisure (or just experiment) to learn the almost limitless number of more subtle and specialized things that are possible. Have fun!

2.1. The Toolbox

Figure 3.4. Screenshot of the Toolbox

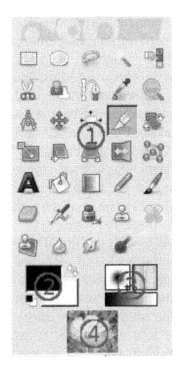

The Toolbox is the heart of GIMP. Here is a quick tour of what you will find there.

Tip

In the Toolbox, as in most parts of GIMP, moving the mouse over something and letting it rest for a moment, usually displays a "tooltip" that describes the thing. Short cut keys are also frequently shown in the tooltip. In many cases, you can hover the mouse over an item and press the **F1** key to get help about the thing that is underneath the mouse.

By default, only the Foreground-background icon is visible. You can add Brush-Pattern-Gradient icons and Active Image icon through Edit → Preferences → Toolbox: Tools configuration.

1. *Tool icons:* These icons are buttons which activate tools for a wide variety of purposes: selecting parts of images, painting an image, transforming an image, etc. Section 1, **"The Toolbox"** gives an overview of how to work with tools, and each tool is described systematically in the Tools chapter.
2. *Foreground/Background colors:* The color areas here show you GIMP's current foreground and background colors, which come into play in many operations. Clicking on either one of them brings up a color selector dialog that allows you to change to a different color. Clicking on the double-headed arrow swaps the two colors, and clicking on the small symbol in the lower left corner resets them to black and white.
3. *Brush/Pattern/Gradient:* The symbols here show you GIMP's current selections for: the Paintbrush, used by all tools that allow you to paint on the image ("painting" includes operations like erasing and smudging, by the way); for the Pattern, which is used in filling selected areas of an image; and for the Gradient, which comes into play whenever an operation requires a smoothly varying range of colors. Clicking on any of these symbols brings up a dialog window that allows you to change it.
4. *Active Image:* In GIMP, you can work with many images at once, but at any given moment, only one image is the "active

image". Here you find a small iconic representation of the active image. Click the icon to display a dialog with a list of the currently open images, click an image in the dialog to make it active. Usually, you click an image window in multi-window mode, or an image tab in single-window mode, to make it the active image.

You can "Drop to an XDS file manager to save the image". XDS is an acronym for "X Direct Save Protocol": an additional feature for the X Window System graphical user interface for Unix-like operating systems.

Note

At every start, GIMP selects a tool (the brush), a color, a brush and a pattern by default, always the same. If you want GIMP to select the last tool, color, brush and pattern you used when quitting your previous session, check the Save input device settings on exit in Preferences/Input Devices.

Tip

The Toolbox window displays "Wilber's eyes" along the top of the dialog. You can get rid of the "Wilber's eyes" by adding the following line to your gimprc file: (toolbox-wilber no). It only affects the toolbox. The eyes in the Image window are only visible when you do not have an open image.

Tip

Drag and drop an image from a file browser into the Toolbox window to open the image in its own Image window or tab.

2.2. Image Window

GIMP user interface is now available in two modes: multi-window mode (default), and single-window mode (optional, through

Windows → >Single-Window Mode. But, if you quit GIMP with this option enabled, GIMP will open in single mode next time).

In single-window mode, no new window is added: images and dialogs are added in tabs.

When you start GIMP without any image open, the image window seems to be absent in single-window mode, while, in multi-window mode, an image window exists, even if no image is open.

We will begin with a brief description of the components that are present by default in an ordinary image window. Some of the components can be removed by using commands in the View menu.

Figure 3.5. The Image Window in Multi-Window Mode

Figure 3.6. The Image Area in Single-Window Mode

 Note

Despite *Single*-window Mode, we will use "image window" for "image area".

1. *Title Bar:* The Title Bar in an image window without an image displays "GNU Image Manipulating Program". An image window with an image displays the image name and its specifications in the title bar according to the settings in Preference Dialog. The Title Bar is provided by the operating system, not by GIMP, so its appearance is likely to vary with the operating system, window manager, and/or theme — in Linux systems, this title bar has a button to display the image window on all your desktops. You also have this button in toolbox window and layer window.

If you have opened a non-xcf image, it is "(imported)" as a .xcf file and its original name appears in the status bar at the bottom of the image window.

When an image is modified, an asterisk appears in front of title.

2. *Image Menu:* Directly below the Title Bar appears the Menu bar (unless it has been suppressed). The Image Menu provides access to nearly every operation you can perform on an image. You can also right-click on an image to display a pop-up image menu, [1], or by left-clicking on the little "arrow-head" symbol in the upper left corner, called *Menu Button*, described just below. Many menu commands are also associated with keyboard *shortcuts* as shown in the menu. You can define your own custom shortcuts for menu actions, if you enable Use Dynamic Keyboard Shortcuts in the Preferences dialog.
3. *Menu Button:* Click the Menu Button to display the Image Menu in a column, (essential in full screen mode). If you like to use keyboard shortcuts, use **Shift**+**F10** to open the menu.
4. *Ruler:* In the default layout, rulers are shown above and to the left of the image. Use the rulers to determine coordinates within the image. The default unit for rulers is pixels; use the settings described below to use a unit other than pixels.

One of the most important uses of rulers is to create *guides*. Click and drag a ruler into the image to create a guide. A guide is a line that helps you accurately position things—or verify that another line is truly horizontal or vertical. Click and drag a guide to move it. Drag a guide out of the image to delete it; you can always drag another guide into the image. You can even use multiple guides at the same time.

In ruler area, the mouse pointer position is marked with two small arrow-heads pointing vertically and horizontally.

5. *QuickMask Toggle:* The small button in the lower left corner of the image toggles the Quick Mask on and off. When the

Quick Mask is on, the button is outlined in red. See **QuickMask** for more details on this highly useful tool.

6. *Pointer Coordinates:* When the pointer (mouse cursor, if you are using a mouse) is within the image boundaries, the rectangular area in the lower left corner of the window displays the current pointer coordinates. The units are the same as for the rulers.

7. *Units Menu:* Use the Units Menu to change the units used for rulers and several other purposes. The default unit is pixels, but you can quickly change to inches, cm, or several other possibilities using this menu. Note that the setting of "Dot for dot" in the View menu affects how the display is scaled: see **Dot for Dot** for more information.

8. *Zoom Button:* There are a number of ways to zoom the image in or out, but the Zoom Button is perhaps the simplest. You can directly enter a zoom level in the text box for precise control.

9. *Status Area:* The Status Area is at the bottom of the image window. By default, the Status Area displays the original name of the image.xcf file, and the amount of system memory used by the image. Please use Edit → Preferences → Image Windows → Title & Status to customize the information displayed in the Status Area. During time-consuming operations, the status area temporarily shows the running operation and how complete the operation is.

Note

Note that the memory used by the image is very different from the image file size. For instance, a 70Kb .PNG image may occupy 246Kb in RAM when displayed. There are two primary reasons the difference in memory usage. First, a .PNG file is compressed format, and the image is reconstituted in RAM in uncompressed form. Second, GIMP uses extra memory, and copies of the image, for use by the Undo command.

10. *Cancel Button:* During complex time-consuming operations, usually a plug-in, a Cancel button temporarily appears in the lower right corner of the window. Use the Cancel button to stop the operation.

Note

A few plug-ins respond badly to being canceled, sometimes leaving corrupted pieces of images behind.

11. *Navigation Control:* This is a small cross-shaped button at the lower right corner of the image display. Click and hold (do not release the mouse button) on the navigation control to display the Navigation Preview. The Navigation Preview has a miniature view of the image with the displayed area outlined. Use the Navigation Preview to quickly pan to a different part of the image—move the mouse while keeping the button pressed. The Navigation Window is often the most convenient way to quickly navigate around a large image with only a small portion displayed. (If your mouse has a middle-button, click-drag with it to pan across the image).
12. *Inactive Padding Area:* When the image dimensions are smaller than the image window, this padding area separates the active image display and the inactive padding area, so you're able to distinguish between them. You cannot apply any Filters or Operations in general to the inactive area.
13. *Image Display:* The most important part of the image window is, of course, the image display or canvas. It occupies the central area of the window, surrounded by a yellow dotted line showing the image boundary, against a neutral gray background. You can change the zoom level of the image display in a variety of ways, including the Zoom setting described below.
14. *Image Window Resize Toggle:* Without enabling this feature, if you change the size of the image window by click-and-dragging border limits, the image size and zoom does not change. If you make the window larger, for example, then you will see more of the image. If this button is pressed, however,

the image resizes when the window resizes so that (mostly) the same portion of the image is displayed before and after the window is resized.

Tip

Drag and drop an image into the Toolbox window from a file browser to open the image in its own Image window or tab.

Dragging an image file into the Layer dialog adds it to the image as a new layer.

Image size and image window size can be different. You can make image fit window, and vice versa, using two keyboard shortcuts:

- **Ctrl+J**: this command keeps the zoom level; it adapts window size to image size. The Shrink Wrap command does the same.
- **Ctrl+Shift+J**: this command modifies the zoom level to adapt the image display to the window.

Users with an Apple Macintosh and a one button mouse can use **Ctrl** + mouse button instead.

2.3. Dialogs and Docking
2.3.1. Organizing Dialogs

GIMP has great flexibility for arranging dialog on your screen. A "dialog" is a moving window which contains options for a tool or is dedicated to a special task. A "dock" is a container which can hold a collection of persistent dialogs, such as the Tool Options dialog, Brushes dialog, Palette dialog, etc. Docks cannot, however, hold non-persistent dialogs such as the Preferences dialog or an Image window.

GIMP has three default docks:

- the Tool Options dock under the Toolbox in the left panel,

- the Layers, Channels, Paths and Undo dock in the upper part of the right panel,
- the Brushes, Patterns and Gradients dock in the lower part of the right panel.

In these docks, each dialog is in its own tab.

In multi-window mode, the Toolbox is a *utility window* and not a dock. In single-window mode, it belongs to the single window.

Use Windows → Dockable Dialogs to view a list of dockable dialogs. Select a dockable dialog from the list to view the dialog. If the dialog is available in a dock, then it is made visible. If the dialog is not in a dock, the behavior is different in multi and single window modes:

- In multi-window mode, a new window, containing the dialog, appears on the screen.
- In single-window mode, the dialog is automatically docked to the Layers-Undo dock as a tab.

You can click-and-drag a tab and drop it in the wanted place:

- either in the tab bar of a dock, to integrate it in the dialog group,
- or on a docking bar that appears as a blue line when the mouse pointer goes over a dock border, to anchor the dialog to the dock.

In multi-window mode, you can also click on the dialog title and drag it to the wanted place.

Figure 3.7. Integrating a new dialog in a dialog group

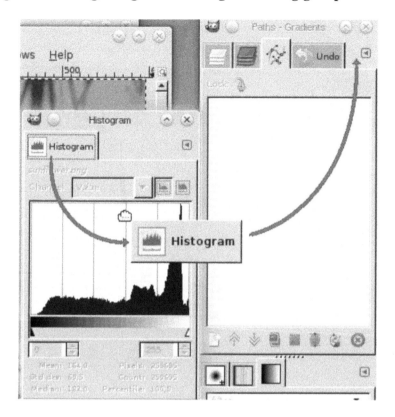

Here, in multi-window mode, the Histogram dialog was dragged to the tab bar of the Layers-Undo dock.

Figure 3.8. Anchoring a dialog to a dock border

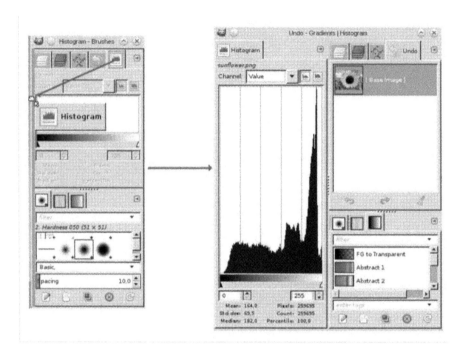

The Histogram dialog dragged to the left vertical docking bar of the right panel and the result: the dialog anchored to the left border of the right panel. This dialog now belongs to the right panel.

So, you can arrange dialogs in a *multi-column* display, interesting if you work with two screens, one for dialogs, the other for images.

 Tip

Press **TAB** in an Image window to toggle the visibility of the docks. This is useful if the docks hide a portion of the image Window. You can quickly hide all the docks, do your work, then display all the docs again. Pressing **TAB** inside a dock to navigate through the dock.

2.3.2. Tab Menu

Figure 3.9. A dialog in a dock, with the Tab menu button highlighted.

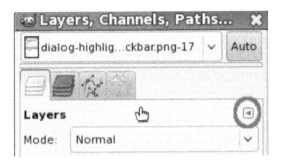

In each dialog, you can access a special menu of tab-related operations by pressing the Tab Menu button, as highlighted in the figure above. Exactly which commands are shown in the menu depends on the active dialog, but they always include operations for creating new tabs, closing or detaching tabs.

Figure 3.10. The Tab menu of the Layers dialog.

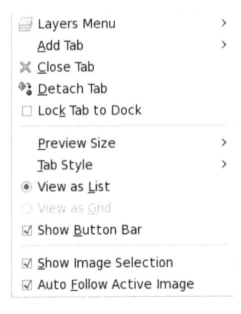

The Tab menu gives you access to the following commands:

Context Menu

> At the top of each Tab menu, an entry opens the dialog's context menu, which contains operations specific to that particular type of dialog. For example, the context menu for the Layers tab is Layers Menu, which contains a set of operations for manipulating layers.

Add Tab

> Add Tab opens into a submenu allowing you to add a large variety of dockable dialogs as new tabs.

Figure 3.11. "Add tab" sub-menu

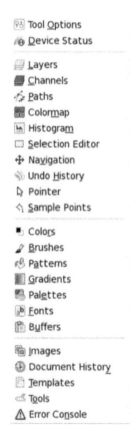

Close Tab

> Close the dialog. Closing the last dialog in a dock causes the dock itself to close.

Detach Tab

> Detach the dialog from the dock, creating a new dock with the detached dialog as its only member. It has the same effect as dragging the tab out of the dock and releasing it at a location where it cannot be docked.
>
> It's a way to create a paradoxical new window in single-window mode!
>
> If the tab is locked, this menu item is insensitive and grayed out.

Lock Tab to Dock

> Prevent the dialog from being moved or detached. When activated, Detach Tab is insensitive and grayed out.

Preview Size

> **Figure 3.12. Preview Size submenu of a Tab menu.**
>
>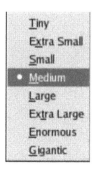

Many, but not all, dialogs have Tab menus containing a Preview Size option, which opens into a submenu giving a list of sizes for the items in the dialog (see the figure above). For example, the Brushes dialog shows pictures of all available brushes: the Preview Size determines how large the pictures are. The default is Medium.

Tab Style

Figure 3.13. Tab Style submenu of a Tab menu.

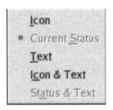

Available only when multiple dialogs are in the same dock, Tab Style opens a submenu allowing you to choose the appearance of the tabs at the top (see the figure above). There are five choices, not all are available for every dialog:

Icon

Use an icon to represent the dialog type.

Current Status

Is only available for dialogs that allows you to select something, such as a brush, pattern, gradient, etc. Current Status shows a representation of the currently selected item in the tab top.

Text

> Use text to display the dialog type.

Icon and Text

> Using both an icon and text results in wider tabs.

Status and Text

> Show the currently selected item and text with the dialog type.

View as List; View as Grid

> These entries are shown in dialogs that allow you to select an item from a set: brushes, patterns, fonts, etc. You can choose to view the items as a vertical list, with the name of each beside it, or as a grid, with representations of the items but no names. Each has its advantages: viewing as a list gives you more information, but viewing as a grid allows you to see more possibilities at once. The default for this varies across dialogs: for brushes and patterns, the default is a grid; for most other things, the default is a list.
>
> You can also use a list search field:

Figure 3.14. The list search field.

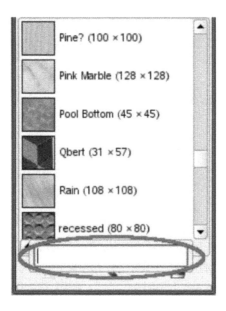

Use **Ctrl+F** to open the list search field. An item must be selected for this command to be effective.

The list search field automatically closes after five seconds if you do nothing.

 Note

The search field shortcut is also available for the tree-view you get in the "Brush", "Font" or "Pattern" option of several tools.

Show Button Bar

Some dialogs display a button bar on the bottom of the dialog; for example, the Patterns, Brushes, Gradients, and Images dialogs. This is a toggle. If it is checked, then the Button Bar is displayed.

Figure 3.15. Button Bar on the Brushes dialog.

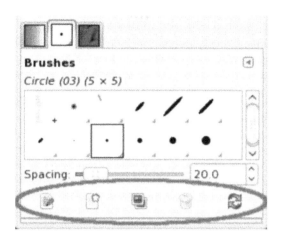

Show Image Selection

> This option is available in multi-window mode only. This is a toggle. If it is checked, then an Image Menu is shown at the top of the dock:

Figure 3.16. A dock with an Image Menu highlighted.

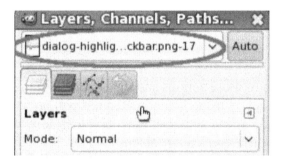

> It is not available for dialogs docked below the Toolbox. This option is interesting only if you have several open images on your screen.

Auto Follow Active Image

55

This option is available in multi-window mode only. This option is also interesting only if you have several images open on your screen. Then, the information displayed in a dock is always that of the selected image in the Image Selection drop-down list. If the Auto Follow Active Image is disabled, the image can be selected only in the Image Selection. If enabled, you can also select it by activating the image directly (clicking on its title bar).

3. Undoing

Almost anything you do to an image in GIMP can be undone. You can undo the most recent action by choosing Edit → Undo from the image menu, but this is done so frequently that you really should memorize the keyboard shortcut, **Ctrl+Z**.

Undoing can itself be undone. After having undone an action, you can *redo* it by choosing Edit → Redo from the image menu, or use the keyboard shortcut, **Ctrl+Y**. It is often helpful to judge the effect of an action by repeatedly undoing and redoing it. This is usually very quick, and does not consume any extra resources or alter the undo history, so there is never any harm in it.

> **Caution**
>
> If you undo one or more actions and then operate on the image in any way except by using Undo or Redo, it will no longer be possible to redo those actions: they are lost forever. The solution to this, if it creates a problem for you, is to duplicate the image and then test on the copy. (Do *Not* test the original, because the undo/redo history is not copied when you duplicate an image.)

If you often find yourself undoing and redoing many steps at a time, it may be more convenient to work with the **Undo History dialog**, a dockable dialog that shows you a small sketch of each point in the

Undo History, allowing you to go back or forward to that point by clicking.

Undo is performed on an image-specific basis: the "Undo History" is one of the components of an image. GIMP allocates a certain amount of memory to each image for this purpose. You can customize your Preferences to increase or decrease the amount, using the **Environment** page of the Preferences dialog. There are two important variables: the *minimal number of undo levels*, which GIMP will maintain regardless of how much memory they consume, and the *maximum undo memory*, beyond which GIMP will begin to delete the oldest items from the Undo History.

Note

Even though the Undo History is a component of an image, it is not saved when you save the image using GIMP's native XCF format, which preserves every other image property. When the image is reopened, it will have an empty Undo History.

GIMP's implementation of Undo is rather sophisticated. Many operations require very little Undo memory (e.g., changing visibility of a layer), so you can perform long sequences of them before they drop out of the Undo History. Some operations, such as changing layer visibility, are *compressed*, so that doing them several times in a row produces only a single point in the Undo History. However, there are other operations that may consume a lot of undo memory. Most filters are implemented by plug-ins, so the GIMP core has no efficient way of knowing what changed. As such, there is no way to implement Undo except by memorizing the entire contents of the affected layer before and after the operation. You might only be able to perform a few such operations before they drop out of the Undo History.

3.1. Things That Cannot be Undone

Most actions that alter an image can be undone. Actions that do not alter the image generally cannot be undone. Examples include saving the image to a file, duplicating the image, copying part of the image to the clipboard, etc. It also includes most actions that affect the image display without altering the underlying image data. The most important example is zooming. There are, however, exceptions: toggling QuickMask on or off can be undone, even though it does not alter the image data.

There are a few important actions that do alter an image but cannot be undone:

Closing the image

> The Undo History is a component of the image, so when the image is closed and all of its resources are freed, the Undo History is gone. Because of this, unless the image has not been modified since the last time it was saved, GIMP always asks you to confirm that you really want to close the image. (You can disable this in the **Environment** page of the Preferences dialog; if you do, you are assuming responsibility for thinking about what you are doing.)

Reverting the image

> "Reverting" means reloading the image from the file. GIMP actually implements this by closing the image and creating a new image, so the Undo History is lost as a consequence. Because of this, if the image is unclean, GIMP asks you to confirm that you really want to revert the image.

"Pieces" of actions

> Some tools require you to perform a complex series of manipulations before they take effect, but only allow you to undo the whole thing rather than the individual elements. For example, the Intelligent Scissors require you to create a closed path by clicking at multiple points in the image, and then clicking inside the path to create a selection. You cannot undo the individual clicks: undoing after you are finished takes you all the way back to the starting point. For another example, when you are working with the Text tool, you cannot undo

individual letters, font changes, etc.: undoing after you are finished removes the newly created text layer.

Filters, and other actions performed by plugins or scripts, can be undone just like actions implemented by the GIMP core, but this requires them to make correct use of GIMP's Undo functions. If the code is not correct, a plugin can potentially corrupt the Undo History, so that not only the plugin but also previous actions can no longer properly be undone. The plugins and scripts distributed with GIMP are all believed to be set up correctly, but obviously no guarantees can be given for plugins you obtain from other sources. Also, even if the code is correct, canceling a plugin while it is running may corrupt the Undo History, so it is best to avoid this unless you have accidentally done something whose consequences are going to be very harmful.

4. Common Tasks

This tutorial is based on text Copyright © 2004 Carol Spears. The original tutorial can be found online: **TUT02**.

4.1. Intention

GIMP is a powerful image editing program with many options and tools. However, it is also well suited for smaller tasks. The following tutorials are meant for those who want to achieve these common tasks without having to learn all the intricacies of GIMP and computer graphics in general.

Hopefully, these tutorials will not only help you with your current task, but also get you ready to learn more complex tools and methods later, when you have the time and inspiration.

All you need to know to start this tutorial, is how to find and open your image. (File → Open from the Image window).

4.2. Change the Size of an Image for the screen

You have a huge image, possibly from a digital camera, and you want to resize it so that it displays nicely on a web page, online board or email message.

Figure 3.17. Example Image for Scaling

The first thing that you might notice after opening the image, is that GIMP opens the image at a logical size for viewing. If your image is very large, like the sample image, GIMP sets the zoom so that it displays nicely on the screen. The zoom level is shown in the status area at the bottom of the Image window. This does not change the actual image.

The other thing to look at in the title-bar is the mode. If the mode shows as RGB in the title bar, you are fine. If the mode says Indexed or Grayscale, read **page 72, "Change the Mode"**.

Figure 3.18. GIMP Used for Image Scaling

Use Image → Scale Image to open the "Scale Image" dialog. You can right click on the image to open the menu, or use the menu along the top of the Image window. Notice that the "Scale Image" menu item contains three dots, which is a hint that a dialog will be opened.

Figure 3.19. Dialog for Image Scaling in Pixels

The unit of size for the purpose of displaying an image on a screen is the pixel. You can see the dialog has two sections: one for width and height and another for resolution. Resolution applies to printing only and has no effect on the image's size when it is displayed on a monitor or a mobile device. The reason is that different devices have different pixels sizes and so, an image that displays on one device (such as a smartphone) with a certain physical size, might display on other devices (such as an LCD projector) in another size altogether. For the purpose of displaying an image on a screen, you can ignore the resolution parameter. For the same reason, do not use any size unit other than the pixel in the height / width fields.

If you know the desired width, enter it in the dialog at the top where it says Width. This is shown in the figure above. If you don't have such a number in mind, choose an appropriate width for the desired use. Common screen sizes range between 320 pixels for simpler phones, 1024 pixels for a netbook, 1440 for a wide-screen PC display and 1920 pixels for an HD screen. for the purpose of displaying an image on-line, a width of 600 to 800 pixels offers a good compromise.

When you change one of the image's dimensions, GIMP changes the other dimension proportionally. To change the other dimension, see **page 68, "Crop An Image"**. Bear in mind that when you change the two dimensions arbitrarily, the image might become stretched or squashed.

4.3. Change the Size of an Image for print

As discussed before, pixels don't have a set size in the real world. When you set out to print an image on paper, GIMP needs to know how big each pixels is. We use a parameter called resolution to set the ratio between pixels and real-world units such as inches.

By default, most images open with the resolution set to 72. This number was chosen for historical reasons as it was the resolution of screens in the past, and means that when printed, every pixel is 1/72 of an inch wide. When printing images are taken with modern digital cameras, this produces very large but chunky images with visible pixels. What we want to do is tell GIMP to print it with the size we have in mind, but not alter the pixel data so as not to lose quality.

To change the print size use Image → Print Size to open the "Print Size" dialog. Select a size unit you are comfortable with, such as "inches". Set one dimension, and let GIMP change the other one proportionally. Now examine the change in resolution. If the resolution is 300 pixels per Inch or over, the printed image's quality will be very high and pixels will not be noticeable. With a resolution of between 200 and 150 ppi, pixels will be somewhat noticeable, but the image will be fine as long as its not inspected too closely. Values lower than 100 are visibly coarse and should only be used for material that is seen from a distance, such as signs or large posters.

Figure 3.20. Dialog for Setting Print Size

4.4. Compressing Images

Figure 3.21. Example Image for JPEG Saving

If you have images that take up a large space on disk, you can reduce that space even without changing the image dimensions. The best image compression is achieved by using the JPG format, but even if the image is already in this format, you can usually still make it take up less space, as the JPG format has an adaptive compression scheme that allows saving in varying levels of compression. The trade-off is that the less space an image takes, the more detail from the original image you lose. You should also be aware that repeated saving in the JPG format causes more and more image degradation.

To save you image as a JPG file, therefore, use File → Save As to open the "Save As" dialog.

Figure 3.22. "Save As" Dialog

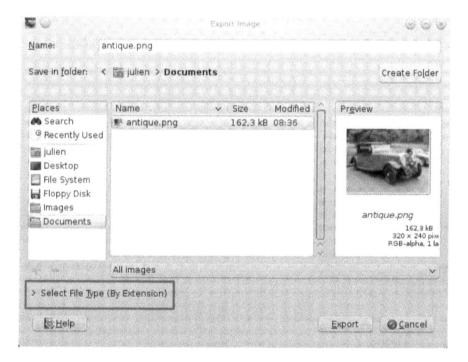

The dialog opens with the file name already typed in the Name box. If the image is not a JPG image, delete the existing extension and type JPG instead, and GIMP will determine the file type from the file extension. Use the file extension list, circled in the figure above, to see the types supported by GIMP. The supported extensions change depending on your installed libraries. If GIMP complains, or if

"JPEG" is grayed out in the Extensions menu, cancel out of everything and step through **page 72, "Change the Mode"**. Once you have done this, click Save. This opens the "Save as" " JPEG dialog that contains the quality control.

The "Save as JPEG" dialog uses default values that reduce size while retaining good visual quality; this is the safest and quickest thing to do.

Figure 3.23. "Save as JPEG" dialog with poor quality.

Reduce the image Quality to make the image even smaller. Reduced quality degrades the image, so be certain to check "Show preview in image window" to visually gauge the degradation. As shown in the figure above, a Quality setting of 10 produces a very poor quality image that uses very little disk space. The figure below shows a more reasonable image. A quality of 75 produces a reasonable image using much less disk space, which will, in turn, load much faster on a web page. Although the image is somewhat degraded, it is acceptable for the intended purpose.

Figure 3.24. Dialog for Image Saving as JPEG

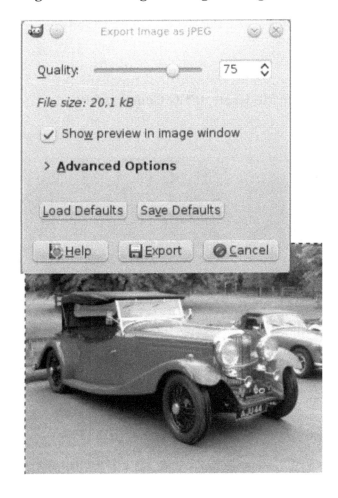

Finally, here is a comparison of the same picture with varying degrees of compression:

Quality: 10; Size: 3.5 KiloBytes   Quality: 40; Size: 9.3 KiloBytes

Figure 3.26. Examples for Moderate JPEG Compression

Quality: 70; Size: 15.2 KiloBytes   Quality: 100; Size: 72.6 KiloBytes

4.5. Crop An Image

Figure 3.27. Example Image for Cropping

Source image   Image after cropping

There are many reasons to crop an image; for example, fitting an image to fill a frame, removing a portion of the background to emphasize the subject, etc. There are two methods to activate the crop tool. Click the ✎ button in the Toolbox, or use Tools → Transform Tools → Crop in the image window. This changes the cursor and allow you to click and drag a rectangular shape. The button in the toolbox is the easiest way to get to any of the tools.

Figure 3.28. Select a Region to Crop

Click on one corner of the desired crop area and drag your mouse to create the crop rectangle. You don't have to be accurate as you can change the exact shape of the rectangle later.

Figure 3.29. Dialog for Cropping

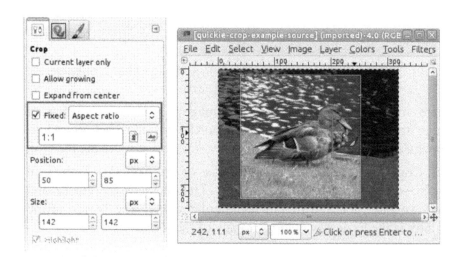

After completing the click and drag motion, a rectangle with special regions is shown on the canvas. As the cursor is moved over the different areas of the selected crop area, the cursor changes. You can then drag the rectangle's corners or edges to change the dimensions of the selected area. As shown in the figure above, as the crop area is resized, the dimensions and ratio are shown in the status bar. If you would like to crop the image in a specific aspect ratio, such as a square, make sure the tool options are visible (Windows → Dockable Dialogs → Tool Options). In the Tool Options dockable, check the mark next to Fixed and make sure the drop-down box next to it is set to Aspect Ratio. You can now type the desired aspect ratio on the text box below, such as "1:1". You also have controls to change the aspect from landscape to portrait. After you set the aspect ratio, drag one of the corners of the crop rectangle to update it. The rectangle changes to the chosen ratio, and when you drag it should maintain that ratio.

4.6. Find Info About Your Image

Figure 3.30. Finding Info

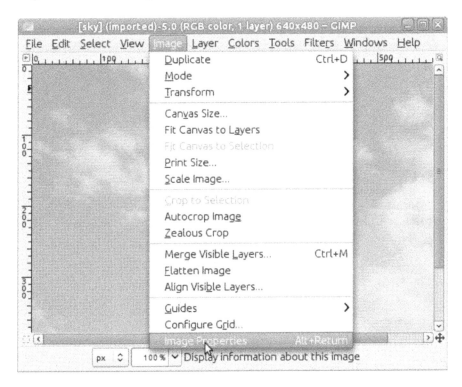

When you need to find out information about your image, Use Image → Image Properties to open the "Image Properties" dialog, which contains information about the image size, resolution, mode and much more.

Figure 3.31. "Image Properties" Dialog

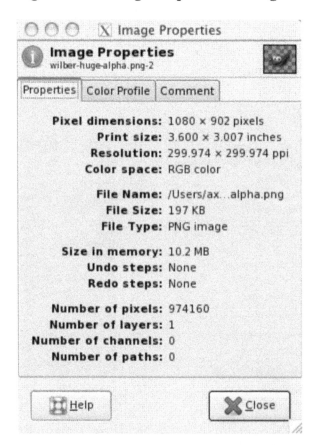

4.7. Change the Mode

As with anything else, images come in different kinds and serve different purposes. Sometimes, a small size is important (for web sites) and at other times, retaining a high color depth (e.g., a family portrait) is what you want. GIMP can handle all of this, and more, primarily by converting between three fundamental modes, as seen in this menu. In order to switch your image to one of these modes, you open it and follow that menu and click the mode you want.

Figure 3.32. Dialog for changing the mode

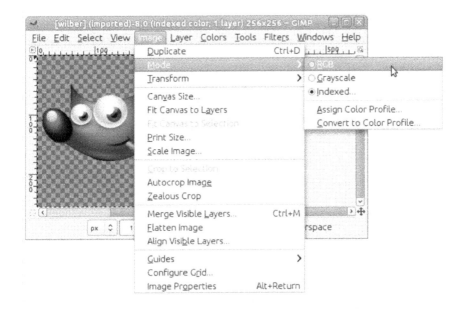

RGB- This is the default mode, used for high-quality images, and able to display millions of colors. This is also the mode for most of your image work including scaling, cropping, and even flipping. In RGB mode, each pixel consists of three different components: R->Red, G->Green, B->Blue. Each of these in turn can have an intensity value of 0-255. What you see at every pixel is an additive combination of these three components.

Indexed- This is the mode usually used when file size is of concern, or when you are working with images with few colors. It involves using a fixed number of colors (256 or less) for the entire image to represent colors. By default, when you change an image to a palleted image, GIMP generates an "optimum palette" to best represent your image.

Figure 3.33. Dialog "Change to Indexed Colors"

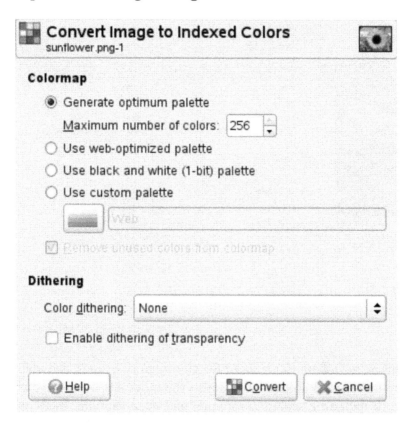

As you might expect, since the information needed to represent the color at each pixel is less, the file size is smaller. However, sometimes, there are options in the various menus that are grayed-out for no apparent reason. This usually means that the filter or option cannot be applied when your image is in its current mode. Changing the mode to RGB, as outlined above, should solve this issue. If RGB mode doesn't work either, perhaps the option you're trying requires your layer to have the ability to be transparent. This can be done just as easily via Layer → Transparency → Add Alpha Channel.

Figure 3.34. Add Alpha Channel

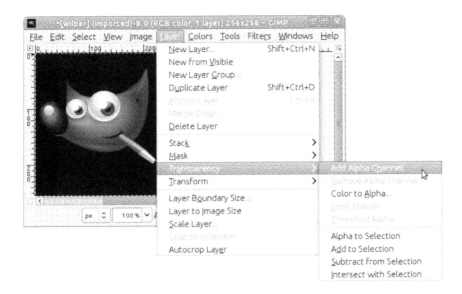

Grayscale- Grayscale images have only shades of gray. This mode has some specific uses and takes less space on the hard drive in some formats, but is not recommended for general use as reading it is not supported by many applications.

There is no need to convert an image to a specific mode before saving it in your favorite format, as GIMP is smart enough to properly export the image.

4.8. Flip An Image

Use this option when you need the person in the photo looking in the other direction, or you need the top of the image to be the bottom. Use Tools → Transform Tools → Flip, or use the ![] button on the toolbox. After selecting the flip tool from the toolbox, click inside the canvas. Controls in the Tool Options dockable let you switch between Horizontal and Vertical modes.

Figure 3.35. Dialog "Flip an Image"

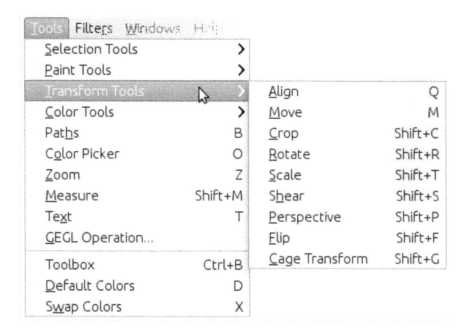

After selecting the flip tool from the toolbox, click inside the canvas. The tool flips the image horizontally. Use the options dialog to switch between horizontal and vertical. If it is not already displayed in the dock under the toolbox, double click the toolbox button. You can also use the **Ctrl** key to switch between horizontal and vertical.

In the images below, all possible flips are demonstrated:

4.9. Rotate An Image

Figure 3.36. Example Image to Flip

Source image

Horizontal flipped image

Vertical flipped image

Horizontal and vertical flipped image

Figure 3.37. Menu for "Rotate An Image"

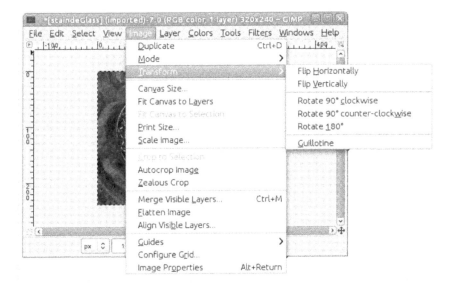

Images that are taken with digital cameras sometimes need to be rotated. To do this, use Image → Transform → Rotate 90° clockwise (or counter-clockwise). The images below demonstrate a 90 degrees CCW rotation.

Figure 3.38. Example for "Rotate An Image"

Source image   Rotated image 90 degree CCW

4.10. Separating an Object From Its Background

Figure 3.39. Object with Background

Sometimes you need to separate the subject of an image from its background. You may want to have the subject on a flat color, or keep the background transparent so you can use it on an existing background, or any other thing you have in mind. To do this, you must first use GIMP's selection tools to draw a selection around your subject. This is not an easy task, and selecting the correct tool is crucial. You have several tools to accomplish this.

The "Free Select Tool" allows you to draw a border using either freehand or straight lines. Use this when the subject has a relatively simple shape.

Figure 3.40. Free Select Tool

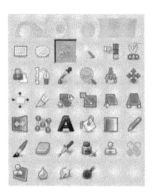

The "Intelligent Scissors Select Tool" lets you select a freehand border and uses edge-recognition algorithms to better fit the border around the object. Use this when the subject is complex but distinct enough against its current background.

Figure 3.41. Intelligent Scissors Select Tool

The "Foreground Select Tool" lets you mark areas as "Foreground" or "Background" and refines the selection automatically.

Figure 3.42. Foreground Select Tool

Once you have selected your subject successfully, use Select →
Invert. Now, instead of the subject, the background is selected. What
you do now depends on what you intended to do with the background.

- To fill the background with a single color:

    Click the foreground color swatch (the top left of the two
    overlapping colored rectangles) in the toolbox and select the
    desired color. Next, use **"Bucket Fill"** to replace the
    background with your chosen color.

Figure 3.43. Result of Adding a Plain Color Background

- To make a transparent background:

  Use Layer → Transparence → Add Alpha Channel to add an alpha channel. Next, use Edit Clear or hit the **Del** key on the keyboard to remove the background. Please note that only a small subset of file formats support transparent areas. Your best bet is to save your image as PNG.

  Figure 3.44. Result of Adding a Transparent Background

- To make a black-and-white background while keeping the subject in color:

  Use Colors → Desaturate. In the dialog that opens, cycle between the modes and select the best-looking one, then click OK.

Figure 3.45. Result of Desaturating the Background

5. How to Draw Straight Lines

This tutorial is based on Text and images Copyright © 2002 Seth Burgess. The original tutorial can be found in the Internet TUT01.

5.1. Intention

Figure 3.46. Example of straight lines

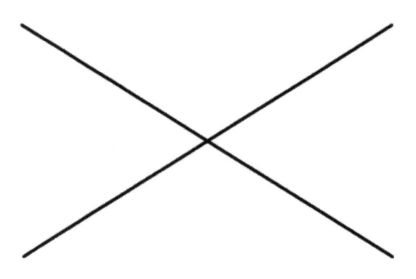

This tutorial shows you how to draw straight lines with GIMP. Forcing a line to be straight is a convenient way to deal with the imprecision of a mouse or tablet, and to take advantage of the power of a computer to make things look neat and orderly. This tutorial doesn't use Straight Lines for complex tasks; it's intended to show how you can use it to create quick and easy straight lines.

1. **Preparations**

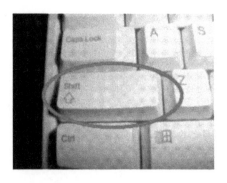

The invention called the typewriter introduced the **Shift** Key. You generally have 2 of them on your keyboard. They look something like the figure above. The keys are located on the left and right sides of your keyboard. The mouse was invented by Douglas C. Engelbart in 1970. These come in different varieties, but always have at least one button.

2. **Creating a Blank Drawable**

Figure 3.48. New image

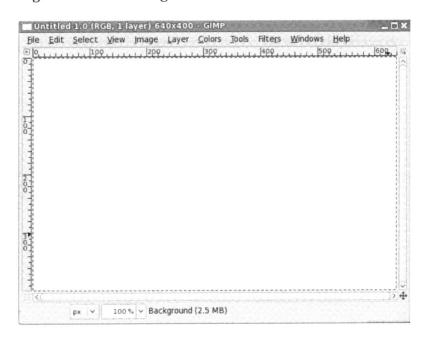

First, create a new image. Any size will do. Use File → New to create a new image.

3. **Choose a Tool**

Figure 3.49. Paint tools in the toolbox

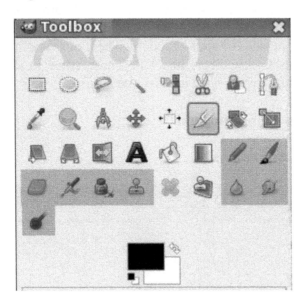

Any of the red-highlighted tools on the above toolbox can do lines.

4. **Create a Starting Point**

   Figure 3.50. Starting point

Click on the paintbrush in the toolbox. Click in the image where you want a line to start or end. A single dot will appear on the screen. The size of this dot represents the current brush size, which you can change in the Brush Dialog. Now, let's start drawing a line. Hold down the **Shift** key, and keep it down.

5. **Drawing the Line**

Figure 3.51. Drawing the line

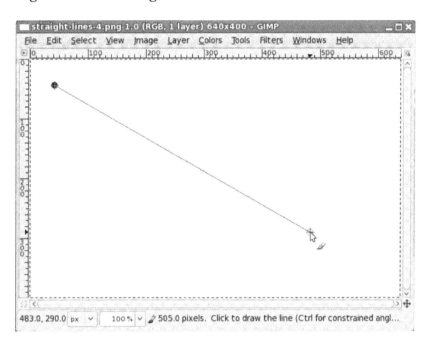

After you have a starting point and while pressing the **Shift**, you will see a straight line that follows the cursor. Press the first button on the Mouse (the leftmost one usually) and let it go. During that whole "click" of the Mouse button, you need to keep the **Shift** Key held down.

6. **Final**

87

Figure 3.52. Final Image

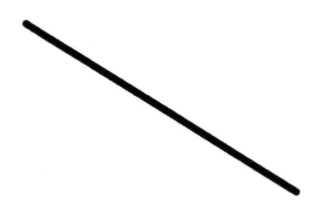

This is a powerful feature. You can draw straight lines with any of the draw tools. You can even draw more lines at the end of this one. Our last step is to let go of the **Shift** key. And there you have it. Some more examples are shown below. Happy GIMPing!

5.2. Examples

Figure 3.53. Examples I

Check Use color from gradient

Select the clone tool and set the source to "Maple Leaves" pattern.

Figure 3.54. Examples II

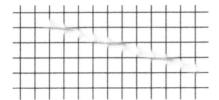 

Use Filters → Render → Pattern → Grid create a grid. Use the Smudge Tool to draw a line with a slightly larger brush.

Use Filters → Render → Clouds → to Plasma to create the cool plasma cloud. Use the Erase Tool with a square brush to draw a line.

Figure 3.55. Example III

Use the rectangle select tool to select a rectangle, and then fill the selection with a light blue color. Select the dodge/burn tool. Set the type to Dodge and paint along the top and left side using an appropriately sized brush. Set the type to Burn and paint along the right and bottom.

CHAPTER 4. GETTING UNSTUCK

1. Getting Unstuck

1.1. Stuck!

All right, okay: you're stuck. You're trying to use one of the tools on an image, and nothing is happening, and nothing you try makes any difference. Your fists are starting to clench, and your face is starting to feel warm. Are you going to have to kill the program, and lose all your work? This sucks!

Well, hold on a second. This happens pretty frequently, even to people who've used GIMP for a long time, but generally the cause is not so hard to figure out (and fix) if you know where to look. Let's be calm, and go through a checklist that will probably get you GIMPing happily again.

1.2. Common Causes of GIMP Non-Responsiveness

1.2.1. There is a floating selection

Figure 4.1. Layers dialog showing a floating selection.

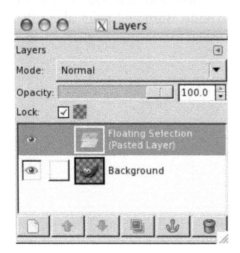

How to tell: If there is a floating selection, many actions are impossible until the floating section is anchored. To check, look at the Layers dialog (making sure it's set to the image you're working on) and see whether the top layer is called "Floating Selection".

How to solve: Either anchor the floating selection, or convert it into an ordinary (non-floating) layer.

1.2.2. The selection is hidden

Figure 4.2. Unstuck show selection menu

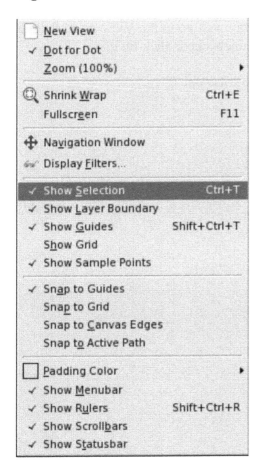

In the View menu, make sure that "Show Selection" is checked.

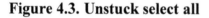

How to tell: If this is the problem, merely reading this will already have made you realize it, probably, but to explain in any case: sometimes the flickering line that outlines the selection is annoying because it makes it hard to see important details of the image, so GIMP gives you the option of hiding the selection, by unchecking Show Selection in the View menu. It is easy to forget that you have done this, though.

How to fix: If this hasn't rung any bells, it isn't the problem, and if it has, you probably know how to fix it, because it doesn't happen unless you explicitly tell it to; but anyway: just go to the View menu for the image and, if Show Selection is unchecked, click on it.

1.2.3. You are acting outside of the selection

Figure 4.3. Unstuck select all

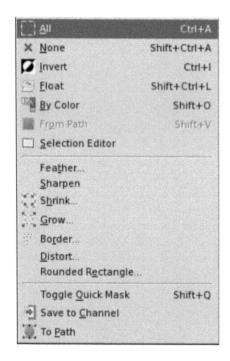

Click "All" in the Select menu to make sure that everything is selected.

How to fix: If doing this has destroyed a selection that you wanted to keep, hit **Ctrl+Z** (undo) a couple of times to restore it, and then we'll figure out what the problem is. There are a couple of possibilities. If you couldn't see any selection, there may have been a very tiny one, or even one that contained no pixels. If this was the case, it surely is not a selection that you wanted to keep, so why have you gotten this far in the first place? If you can see a selection but thought you were inside it, it might be inverted from what you think. The easiest way to tell is to hit the Quick Mask button: the selected area will be clear and the unselected area will be masked. If this was the problem, then you can solve it by toggling Quick Mask off and choosing Invert in the Select menu.

1.2.4. The active drawable is not visible

Figure 4.4. Unstuck layer invisibility

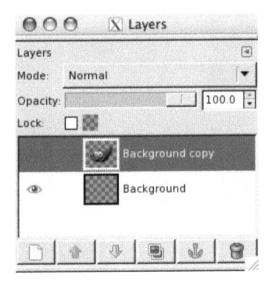

Layers dialog with visibility off for the active layer.

How to tell: The Layers dialog gives you ability to toggle the visibility of each layer on or off. Look at the Layers dialog, and see if the layer you are trying to act on is active (i.e., darkened) and has an eye symbol to the left of it. If not, this is your problem.

How to fix: If your intended target layer is not active, click on it in the Layers dialog to activate it. (If none of the layers are active, the active drawable might be a channel -- you can look at the Channels tab in the Layers dialog to see. This does not change the solution, though.) If the eye symbol does not appear, click in the Layers dialog at the left edge to toggle it: this should make the layer visible.

1.2.5. The active drawable is transparent

Figure 4.5. Unstuck layer transparency

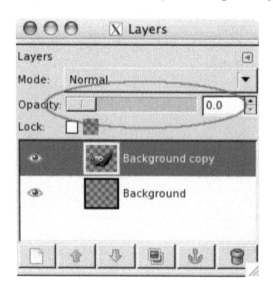

Layers dialog with opacity set to zero for the active layer.

How to tell: When the opacity is set 0 on the layer, you cannot see anything which you draw on it. Look the Opacity slider, and see which side the slider placed at. If it is at the leftmost side, that is your problem.

How to fix: Move the slider.

1.2.6. *You are trying to act outside the layer*

How to tell: In GIMP, layers don't need to have the same dimensions as the image: they can be larger or smaller. If you try to paint outside the borders of a layer, nothing happens. To see if this is happening, look for a black-and-yellow dashed rectangle that does not enclose the area you're trying to draw at.

How to fix: You need to enlarge the layer. There are two commands at the bottom of the Layer menu that will let you do this: Layer to Image Size, which sets the layer bounds to match the image borders; and Layer Boundary Size, which brings up a dialog that allows you to set the layer dimensions to whatever you please.

1.2.7. *The image is in indexed color mode.*

How to tell: GIMP can handle three different color modes: **RGB(A), Indexed and Grayscale**. The indexed colormode uses a colormap, where all used colors on the image are indexed. The color picker in GIMP however, let you choose RGB colors. That means, if you try to paint with a different color than it is indexed in the colormap, you end up in very undetermined results (e.g. it paints with the wrong color or you can't paint).

How to fix: Always use the RGB Color mode to paint on images. You can verify and select another color mode from the Mode menuitem in the Image menu.

HOW TO GET YOUR COPY OF OUR 939-PAGE FULL COLOR GIMP BOOK.

First, we thank you for choosing GIMP 2.8 because if you didn't there won't be any need for a book like this.

Send an email to *contactucabelbooks@gmail.com* for a copy of the 939-page full color GIMP book.

We will appreciate it if you review this book.

Thank you.

Other GIMP Books by U. C-Abel Books

1. GIMP 2.8 Shortcuts
   ISBN-13: 978-1979461191

2. Painting with GIMP
   ISBN-13: 978-1979982627

3. Brighter Days with GIMP 2.8   - Part I & II
   ISBN-13: 978-1517337179

4. Common Tasks in GIMP 2.8 (Full Colour)   - Part I
   ISBN-13:978-1981102341

5. Becoming a GIMP Wizard   - Part II
   ISBN-13: 978-1981117208

To have a complete GIMP guide, here is what you should buy:

1. Common Tasks in GIMP 2.8 (Full Colour)   - <u>Part I</u>
   ISBN-13:978-1981102341

2. Becoming a GIMP Wizard   - <u>Part II</u>

   And request for the free 939 pages book - <u>Part III</u>

OR

1. Brighter Days with GIMP 2.8   - <u>Part I & II</u>
   ISBN-13: 978-1517337179

   And request for the free 939 pages book - <u>Part III</u>

Lightning Source UK Ltd.
Milton Keynes UK
UKHW02f1835200818
327528UK00028B/1633/P